SPANISH-ENGLISH WORD PUZZLE BOOK

Catherine Bruzzone, Rachel Croxon and Louise Millar

Illustrations by Louise Comfort and Steph Dix
Spanish adviser: Diego Blasco Vázquez

BARRON'S

En la granja

Etiqueta los dibujos. Luego rellena el crucigrama y busca las respuestas en la página 30.

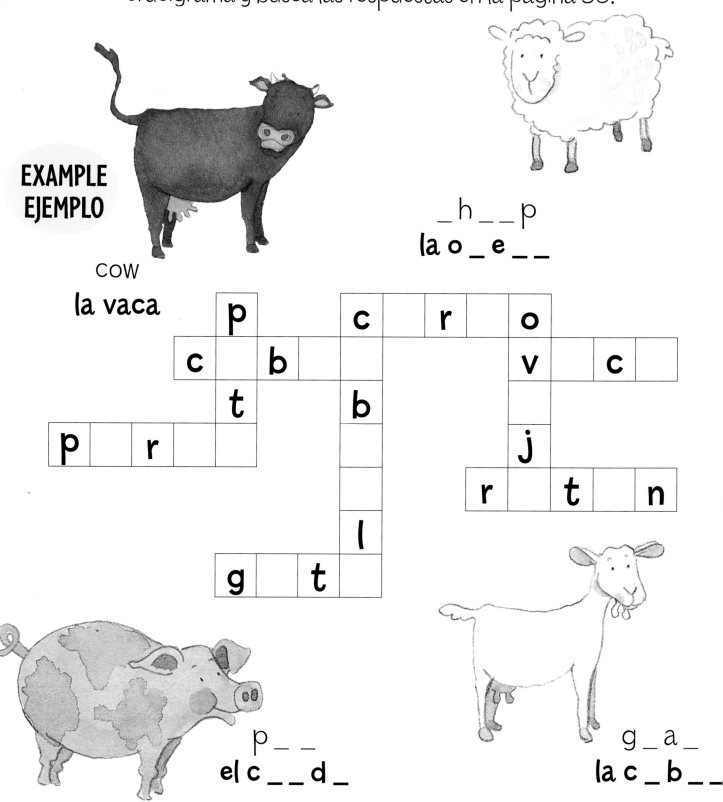

EXAMPLE
EJEMPLO

cow

la vaca

_ h _ _ p

la o _ e _ _

p _ _

el c _ _ d _

g _ a _

la c _ b _ _

On the farm

Label the pictures. Then fill in the crossword and check your answers on page 30.

c _ _
el g _ t _

m _ _ s_
el r _ _ ó _

h _ r _ _
el c _ b _ _ _ _ _

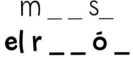

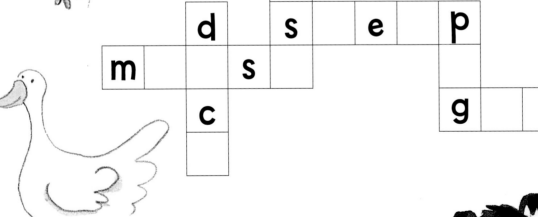

d _ c _
el p _ t _

d _ _
el p _ r _ _

El supermercado

Etiqueta los dibujos. Luego busca las nueve palabras de esta sopa de letras. Respuestas en la página 30.

egg **el huevo**   b_e_d el p_n   m_l_
                                        la l_c_e

w	v	a	r	r	o	z	f	a	h	s
g	k	f	h	a	v	m	k	m	x	g
m	a	n	t	e	q	u	i	l	l	a
x	z	w	s	h	f	k	g	v	h	f
f	ú	f	p	a	s	t	a	x	u	s
v	c	g	c	a	r	n	e	f	e	a
h	a	v	h	f	k	w	h	m	v	x
x	r	s	p	e	s	c	a	d	o	f
a	f	h	a	v	g	h	f	s	k	w
k	h	f	n	s	a	l	e	c	h	e

b_tt_r
la m_n_e q_i_ _a

f_s_
el p_sc_d_

4

The supermarket

Label the pictures and then look for the nine words in this square. Answers on page 30.

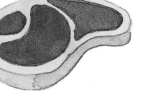

m _ a _
la c _ r _ e

p _ s _ a
la pa _ _ a

x	s	f	z	u	w	o	d	e	v
v	w	u	o	h	d	f	r	g	s
m	e	a	t	r	f	i	z	g	z
d	u	r	d	p	a	s	t	a	w
f	o	h	z	r	v	h	o	s	r
b	u	t	t	e	r	o	w	u	f
b	r	e	a	d	f	v	r	h	d
w	u	z	d	o	u	m	i	l	k
v	h	s	u	g	a	r	c	v	o
r	w	d	o	z	v	f	e	h	z

s _ g _ r
el a _ ú _ a _

r _ c _
el a _ r _ z

5

¿Qué es esto?

Une los puntos y rellena los nombres de estos animales. Respuestas en la página 30.

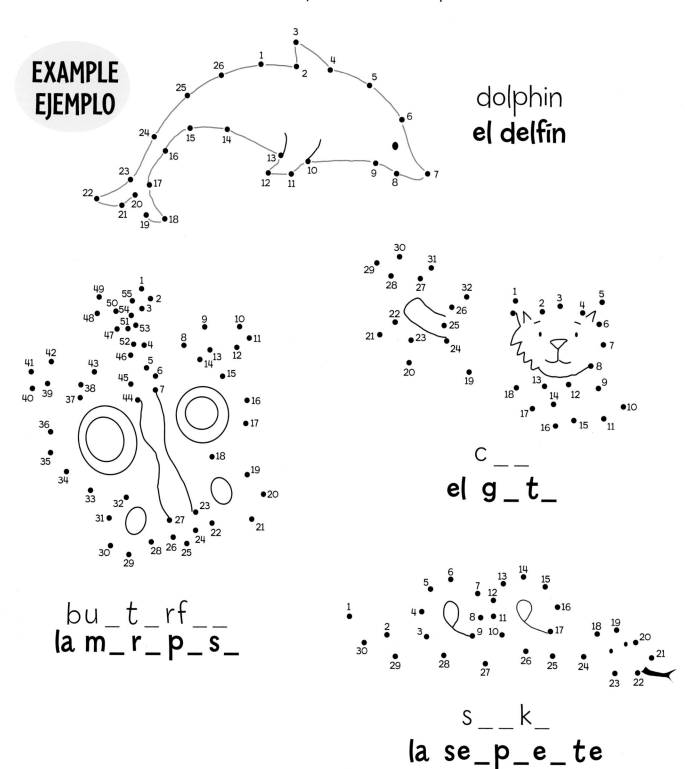

EXAMPLE
EJEMPLO

dolphin
el delfín

c _ _
el g _ t _

bu _ t _ rf _ _
la m _ r _ p _ s _

s _ _ k _
la se _ p _ e _ te

What is this?

Join the dots and complete the names
of these creatures. Answers on page 30.

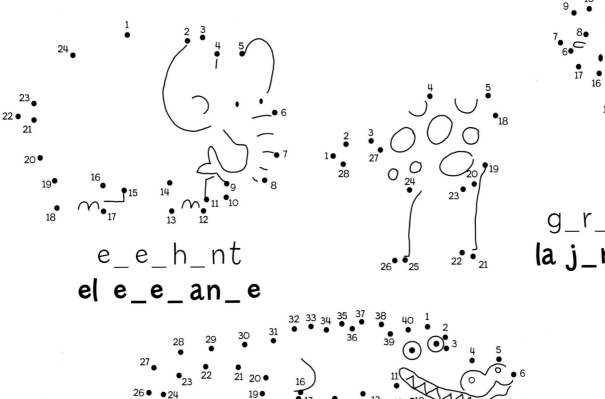

e _ e _ h _ nt

el e_e_an_e

g _ r _ ff _

la j_r_fa

c _ o _ o _ i _ e

el c_c_d_i_o

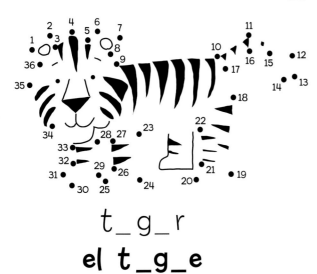

t _ g _ r

el t_g_e

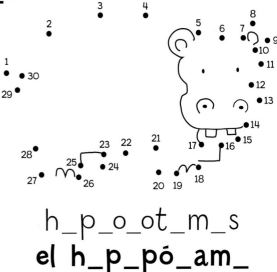

h _ p _ o _ ot _ m _ s

el h_p_pó_am_

En la cocina

Pon las letras que faltan. Las letras de los recuadros forman
la palabra que falta debajo. Respuestas en la página 30.

s☐nk
el fregad_ro

s_u_ep_n
la ca☐e_o☐a

s_ _o☐
la c☐c☐ara

☐ri_ge
el fr_gorífi☐o

el | | | | | | | |

In the kitchen

Fill in the missing letters of the labels. The letters in boxes make up the final missing word below. Answers on page 30.

g_a_s
el v_ _o

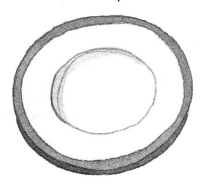

d_ _h
el p☐a_o

s_ o_☐
la c_c☐_a

f_r☐
el te_ _d☐r

Los colores del arco iris

Etiqueta los dibujos. Rellena el crucigrama.
Busca las respuestas en la página 30.

EXAMPLE EJEMPLO

green   **verde**

b _ a _ _   n _ g _ _

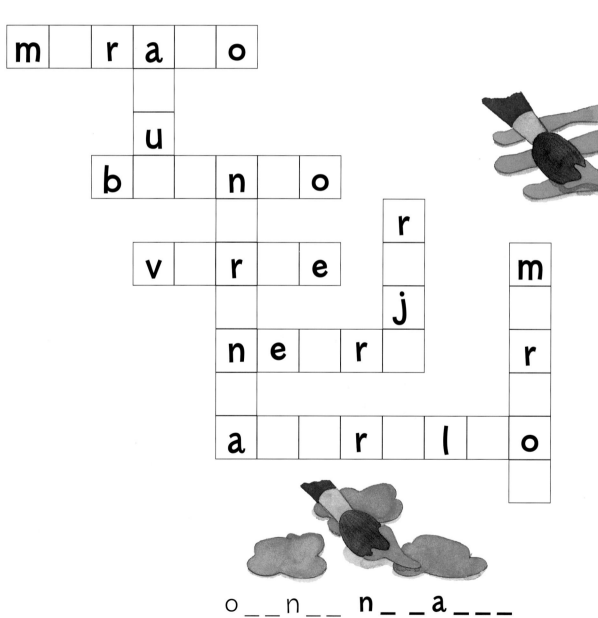

b _ u _
a _ u _

o _ _ n _ _   n _ _ a _ _ _

Colors of the rainbow

Label the pictures. Then fill in the crossword
and check your answers on page 30.

w _ i _ _
b _ a _ _ _

y _ _ l _ _
a _ a _ _ _ _ _

b _ o _ _
m _ r _ _ _

b		y			o			b		a		k
p	r	l			a			o						
e						r								
				g		r	e	n						
w		i			d									

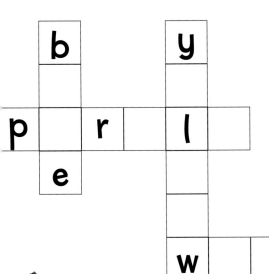

r _ _
r _ j _

p _ r _ _ _
m _ r _ _ _

El mercado

Alguien ha cambiado las etiquetas de la fruta.
¿Puedes escribir los nombres correctos en el espacio
de debajo? Respuestas en la página 30.

los plátanos

bananas

**EXAMPLE
EJEMPLO**

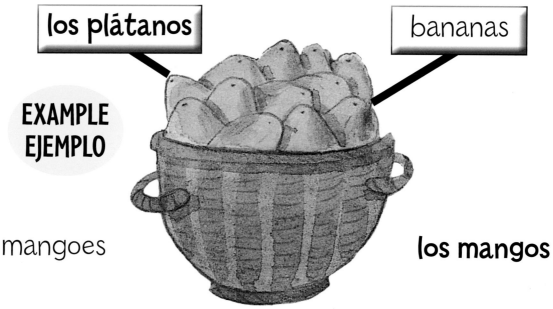

mangoes

los mangos

las naranjas

oranges

las uvas

grapes

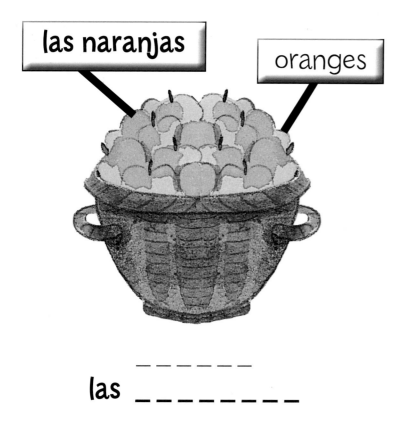

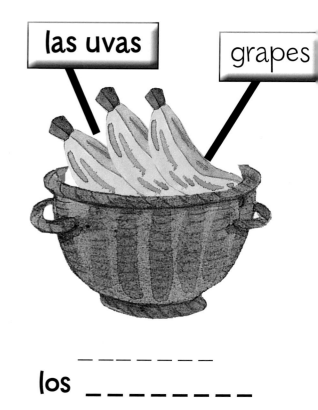

_ _ _ _ _ _ _

las _ _ _ _ _ _ _ _

_ _ _ _ _ _ _

los _ _ _ _ _ _ _ _

The market

Someone has mixed up the labels on the fruit.
Can you write the correct names under each basket of fruit?
Answers on page 30.

las manzanas

apples

_ _ _ _ _ _ _ _
las _ _ _ _ _ _ _ _ _

los mangos

mangoes

las piñas

pineapples

_ _ _ _ _ _ _ _ _ _ _
las _ _ _ _ _

_ _ _ _ _ _
las _ _ _ _

13

En el bosque

Rellena las letras que faltan. Encuentra los nombres de esos nueve animales. Empieza por la letra del círculo y sigue arriba, abajo y de lado. Respuestas en la página 31.

de _ _
el _ie_ _o

_q_i_re_
la a_ _il_a

m	a	r	i	p	n	w	o
o	n	o	m	o	s	a	b
j	e	c	r	c	w	o	r
a	j	n	ó	r	r	k	u
b	o	k	x	s	a	d	g
a	c	d	z	f	m	h	a
r	i	s	ⓞ▸	s	o	x	z
a	e	z	k	o	r	r	o
c	r	v	o	a	r	d	x
s	h	c	s	f	h	i	s
e	d	f	z	x	k	l	d
a	c	s	o	m	a	l	x

bu_t_rf_ _
la m_r_p_s_

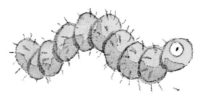

ca_e_p_ _l_r
la _r_g_

14

In the forest

Fill in the missing letters. Find the names of these nine animals and insects starting at the circled letter and going up, down, and sideways. Answers on page 31.

x	c	a	t	t	e	r	p	u
t	y	b	a	s	o	d	i	n
f	l	b	r	z	k	f	l	l
r	w	i	r	a	e	b	c	a
e	f	t	a	n	o	n	v	r
t	n	d	n	d	f	w	l	f
t	o	e	s	ⓑ	r	o	r	o
u	r	e	l	n	c	s	d	x
b	x	r	s	q	u	i	r	s
e	h	a	w	c	o	a	r	o
l	d	f	n	a	d	f	e	a
t	e	e	b	y	l	f	l	w

_ _ x
el _orr_

br_w_ b _ _ r
el _s_ m_rr_n

_a_b_t
el c_n_jo

_ _ y
la m_s_a

b_e_ _e
el _sc_r_b_j_

En el dormitorio

Etiqueta los dibujos. Luego rellena el crucigrama
y busca las respuestas en la página 31.

r_g
la al_o_b_ _ _

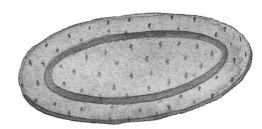

al_ _ _m cl_c_
el d_sp_r_a_o_

v		n		a		a

| | | | | | | c |

a		f		m		r

| | | | | | | m |

d		s	e		t		d		r

t			e		i		i	o

| t |
| t |
| n |
| e |

wi_d_ _
la v_ _t_n_

b_d
la c_ _a

16

In the bedroom

Label the pictures. Then fill in the crossword
and check your answers on page 31.

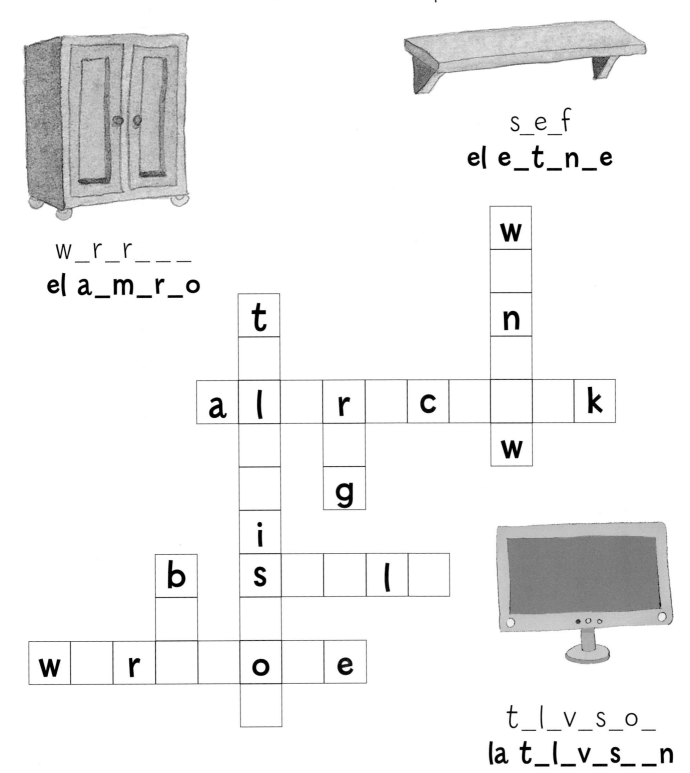

s_e_f
el e_t_n_e

w_r_r _ _ _
el a_m_r_o

t_l_v_s_o_
la t_l_v_s_ _n

Los números y los meses

Escribe el número en cada calendario. Después une cada calendario al mes correcto. Respuestas en la página 31.

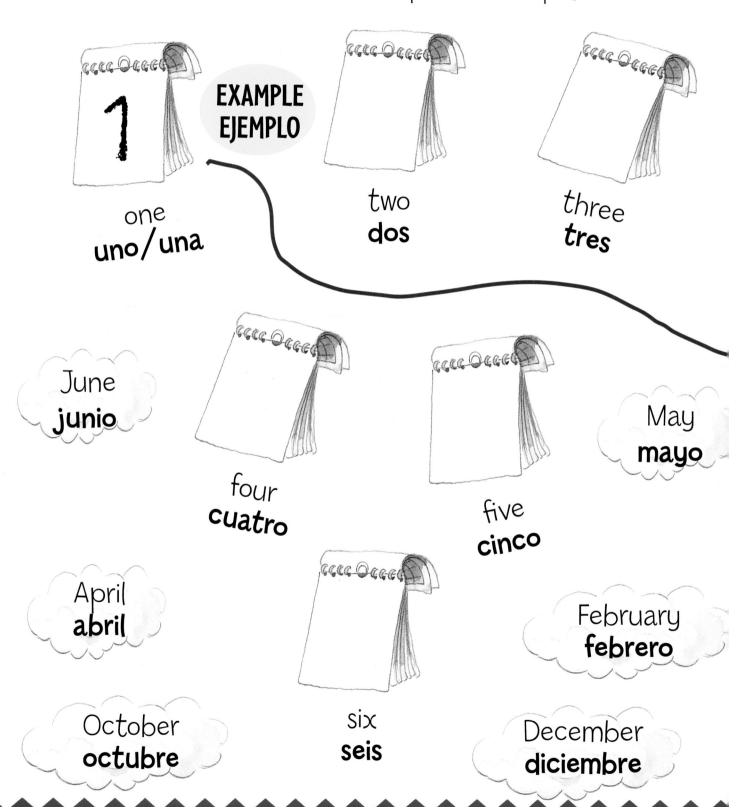

1 EXAMPLE EJEMPLO

one
uno/una

two
dos

three
tres

June
junio

four
cuatro

five
cinco

May
mayo

April
abril

February
febrero

October
octubre

six
seis

December
diciembre

Numbers and months

Fill in the number on the calendar. Then join each calendar to the right month. Answers on page 31.

July
julio

seven
siete

eight
ocho

August
agosto

January
enero

nine
nueve

ten
diez

eleven
once

twelve
doce

September
septiembre

March
marzo

November
noviembre

La ropa

Encuentra las nueve palabras del puzzle
usando la pista de los dibujos.
Respuestas en la página 31.

s_i_t
la f_l_a

d_e_s
el v_s_i_o

x	s	o	m	b	r	e	r	o	t	a
a	b	r	i	g	o	p	u	d	w	x
n	w	u	v	s	f	a	l	d	a	v
w	f	c	g	a	l	n	o	v	k	e
m	c	a	l	c	e	t	i	n	e	s
c	t	m	p	i	j	a	m	a	d	t
n	s	i	r	c	f	l	c	e	f	i
w	e	s	n	d	h	ó	b	t	x	d
r	s	a	u	s	i	n	r	z	d	o
o	z	a	p	a	t	o	s	f	s	h

c_a_
el a_r_g_

s_o_s
los z_p_t_s

p_j_m_s
el p_j_m_

Clothes

Find the nine words in the puzzle using the picture clues.

Answers on page 31.

s _ c _ s

os c_l_e_i_e_

s_i_t

la c_m_s_

s	r	a	n	o	t	w	d	j	e
k	x	u	a	i	k	s	l	d	r
i	c	w	r	s	h	o	e	s	t
r	l	e	c	q	r	s	f	o	g
t	m	d	o	i	e	w	z	c	d
p	a	j	a	m	a	s	e	k	r
c	s	u	t	o	i	h	k	s	e
d	e	f	s	a	z	i	w	o	s
t	r	o	u	s	e	r	s	c	s
a	d	z	x	h	a	t	v	e	k

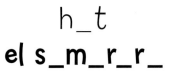

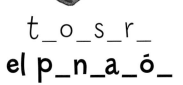

h _ t

el s_m_r_r_

t_o_s_r_

el p_n_a_ó_

En la clase

Numera cada letra del alfabeto de 1 a 26. Así la palabra **clase** es: **3 12 1 19 5**. ¿Cómo se llaman esas cosas de la clase? Respuestas en la página 31.

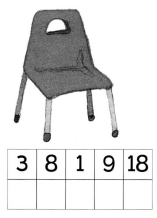

3	8	1	9	18

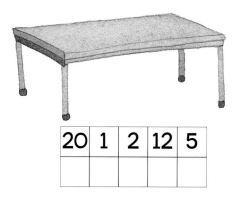

20	1	2	12	5

12	1		19	9	12	12	1

12	1		13	5	19	1

2	15	15	11

5	12		12	9	2	18	15

3	15	12	15	18		16	5	14	3	9	12

5	12		12	1	16	9	26		4	5		3	15	12	15	18

20	5	1	3	8	5	18

12	1		16	18	15	6	5	19	15	18	1

a b c d e f g h i j k l m

In the classroom

Number each letter in the alphabet from 1-26. For example, **classroom** is **3 12 1 19 19 18 15 15 13**. What are the names of these things in the classroom? Answers on page 31.

7	12	21	5

5	12		16	5	7	1	13	5	14	20	15

16	1	16	5	18

5	12		16	1	16	5	12

16	5	14

12	1		16	12	21	13	1

3	15	13	16	21	20	5	18

12	1		3	15	13	16	21	20	1	4	15	18	1

ñ/n   o   p   q   r   s   t   u   v   w   x   y   z

En la playa

Sigue las líneas y reescribe las palabras. Usa las letras de
los cuadritos para formar las palabras para la etiqueta de abajo.
Respuesta en la página 31.

Respuesta en la página 31.

**EXAMPLE
EJEMPLO**

sailboat
el velero

shell
la concha

sea
el mar

fish
el pez

sand
la arena

wave
la ola

seagull
la gaviota

rock
la roca

At the seashore

Follow the tracks and rewrite the words. Use the letters in boxes
to make words for the final missing labels at the bottom of page 25.
Answer on page 31.

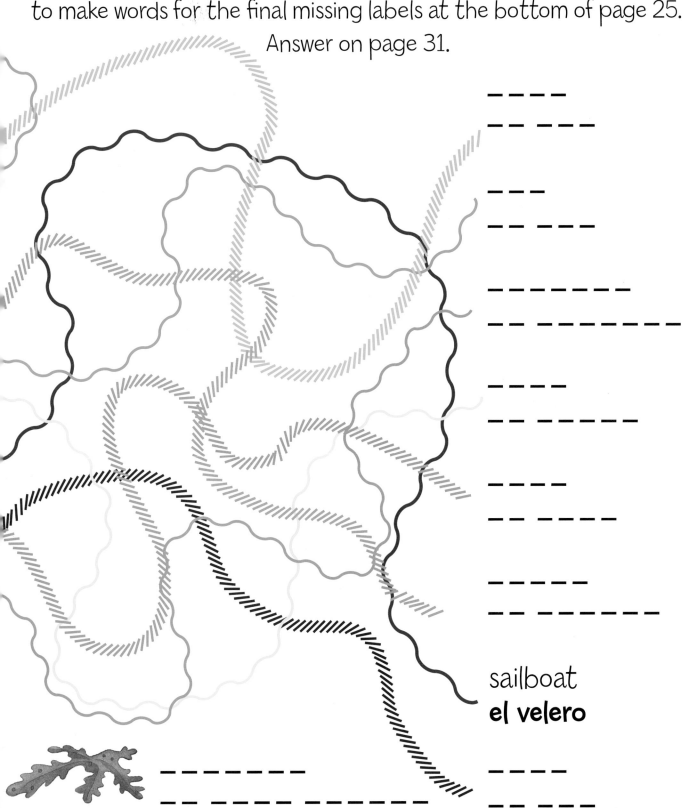

_ _ _ _

_ _ _ _ _ _

_ _ _

_ _ _ _ _

_ _ _ _ _ _ _

_ _ _ _ _ _ _ _

_ _ _ _

_ _ _ _ _ _

_ _ _ _

_ _ _ _ _ _

_ _ _ _ _

_ _ _ _ _ _ _

sailboat
el velero

_ _ _ _ _ _ _ _

_ _ _ _ _ _ _ _ _ _ _ _

_ _ _ _

_ _ _ _ _

Las verduras

Encuentra los nombres de las verduras en la serpiente de palabras y completa las etiquetas. Respuestas en la página 31.

zucchinicarrottomatocelery

EXAMPLE
EJEMPLO

cabbage
la col

p_t_t_
la p_p_

t_m_t_
el t_m_t_

elcalabacinlazanahoriaeltomateelapr

e_g_l_n_
la b_r_n_e_a

c_r_
el m_i_

26

Vegetables

Find the names of the vegetables in the word snake
to complete their labels. Answers on page 31.

l _ t _ u _ e
la l_c_u_a

cabbagecornpotatoeggplantlettuce

c _ l _ r _
el a_i_

z _ _ ch _ n _
el c_l_b_c_n

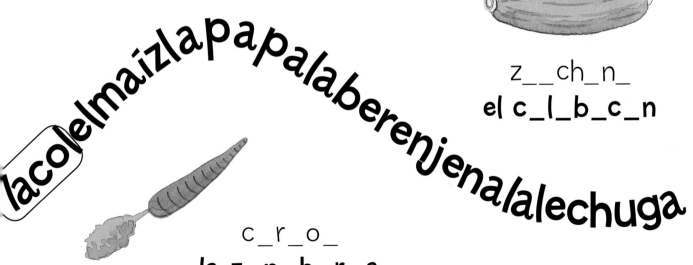

lacolelmaizlapapalaberenjenalalechuga

c _ r _ o _
la z_n_h_r_a

En el campo

Descubre las nueve diferencias entre los dos dibujos.
Las pistas están escritas al revés. Escríbelas bien para
que te ayuden. Respuestas en la página 31.

**EXAMPLE
EJEMPLO**

1. niatnuom   mountain
añatnom al   **la montaña**

2. rewolf   _ _ _ _ _ _
rolf al   _ _ _ _ _ _

3. egdirb   _ _ _ _ _ _
etneup le   _ _ _ _ _ _ _

4. kcud   _ _ _ _
otap le   _ _ _ _ _ _

5. eert   _ _ _ _
lobrá le   _ _ _ _ _ _

In the country

Spot the nine differences between the two pictures.
The clues below are back to front. Rewrite them to
help you find the differences. Answers on page 31.

6. drib _ _ _ _
   orajáp le _ _ _ _ _ _ _ _

7. tibbar _ _ _ _ _ _
   ojenoc le _ _ _ _ _ _ _ _

8. dleif _ _ _ _ _
   odarp le _ _ _ _ _ _ _

9. ssarg _ _ _ _ _
   abreih al _ _ _ _ _ _ _

Las respuestas/Answers

p.2

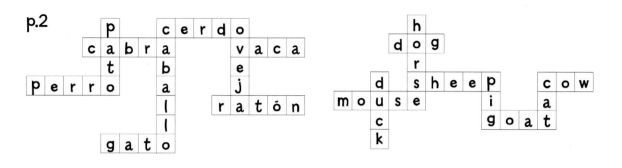

Left crossword:
```
        p       c e r d o
    c a b r a       v a c a
    t       b       e
P e r r o   a       j
            l       r a t ó n
            l
    g a t o
```

Right crossword:
```
            h
        d o g
        r
    d   s h e e p       c o w
m o u s e       i       a
    c           g o a t
    k
```

p.4

Left grid:
```
    a r r o z
m a n t e q u i l l a
  z               h
  ú   p a s t a   u
  c   c a r n e   e
  a               v
  r   p e s c a d o
      a
      n     l e c h e
```

Right grid:
```
                e
              f g
m e a t       i g
          p a s t a
              h
b u t t e r
b r e a d     r
            m i l k
    s u g a r c
            e
```

p.6 – cat/**el gato**, butterfly/**la mariposa**, snake/**la serpiente**, elephant/**el elefante**, giraffe/**la jirafa**, crocodile/**el cocodrilo**, tiger/**el tigre**, hippopotamus/**el hipopótamo**

p.8 – sink/**el fregadero**, saucepan/**la cacerola**, spoon/**la cuchara**, fridge/**el frigorífico**, glass/**el vaso**, dish/**el plato**, stove/**la cocina**, fork/**el tenedor**, knife/**el cuchillo**

p.10

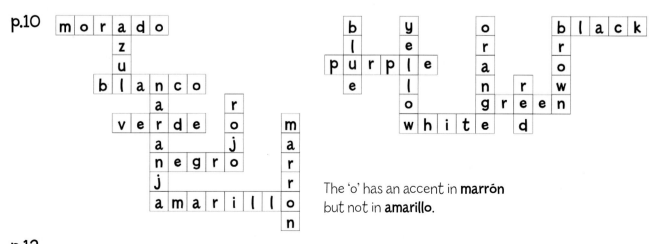

Left crossword:
```
m o r a d o
  z
  u
  b l a n c o
      a       r
      v e r d e       m
      a       j       a
      n e g r o       r
      j               r
      a m a r i l l o
                      n
```

Right crossword:
```
    b       y       o       b l a c k
    l       e       r       r
  p u r p l e       a       o
    e       l       n   r   w
    o       o       g r e e n
    w h i t e       d
```

The 'o' has an accent in **marrón** but not in **amarillo**.

p.12

apples/**las manzanas**, bananas/**los plátanos**, oranges/**las naranjas**, pineapples/**las piñas**, grapes/**las uvas**

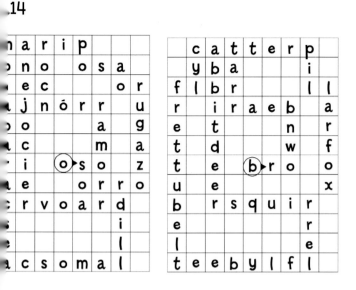

p.14

p.16

The 'o' has an accent in televisión but not in armario.

p.18 – one/**uno**/**una**–January/**enero**, two/**dos**–February/**febrero**, three/**tres**–March/**marzo**, four/**cuatro**–April/**abril**, five/**cinco**–May/**mayo**, six/**seis**–June/**junio**, seven/**siete**–July/**julio**, eight/**ocho**–August/**agosto**, nine/**nueve**–September/**septiembre**, ten/**diez**–October/**octubre**, eleven/**once**–November/**noviembre**, twelve/**doce**–December/**diciembre**

p.20

p.22 – chair/**la silla**, table/**la mesa**, book/**el libro**, color pencil/**el lápiz de color**, teacher/**la profesora**, glue/**el pegamento**, paper/**el papel**, pen/**la pluma**, computer/**la computadora**

p.25 – seaweed/**el alga marina**

p.26 – potato/**la papa**, tomato/**el tomate**, eggplant/**la berenjena**, corn/**el maíz**, lettuce/**la lechuga**, celery/**el apio**, zucchini/**el calabacín**, carrot/**la zanahoria**

p.28 – mountain/**la montaña**, flower/**la flor**, bridge/**el puente**, duck/**el pato**, tree/**el árbol**, bird/**el pájaro**, rabbit/**el conejo**, field/**el prado**, grass/**la hierba**

Lista de palabras/Word list

el abrigo coat
abril April
agosto August
la alfombra rug
el alga marina seaweed
amarillo/amarilla yellow
el apio celery
el árbol tree
el arco iris rainbow
la ardilla squirrel
la arena sand
el armario wardrobe
el arroz rice
el azúcar sugar
azul blue
la berenjena eggplant
blanco/blanca white
el bosque forest
el caballo horse
la cabra goat
la cacerola saucepan
el calabacín zucchini
los calcetines socks
la cama bed
la camisa shirt
el campo country
la carne meat
el cerdo pig
el ciervo deer
cinco five
la clase classroom
la cocina kitchen
la cocina stove
el cocodrilo crocodile
la col cabbage
los colores colors
la computadora computer
la concha shell
el conejo rabbit
cuatro four
la cuchara spoon
el cuchillo knife
el delfín dolphin
el despertador alarm clock
diciembre December
diez ten
doce twelve
el dormitorio bedroom
dos two
el elefante elephant

enero January
el escarabajo beetle
el estante shelf
la falda skirt
febrero February
la flor flower
el fregadero sink
el frigorífico fridge
la fruta fruit
el gato cat
la gaviota seagull
la granja farm
la hierba grass
el hipopótamo hippopotamus
el huevo egg
la jirafa giraffe
julio July
junio June
el lápiz de color color pencil
la leche milk
la lechuga lettuce
el libro book
el maíz corn
el mango mango
la mantequilla butter
la manzana apple
el mar sea
la mariposa butterfly
marrón brown
marzo March
mayo May
el mercado market
el mes month
la mesa table
la montaña mountain
morado/morada purple
la mosca fly
la naranja orange (fruit)
naranja orange (color)
negro/negra black
noviembre November
nueve nine
el número number
ocho eight
octubre October
la ola wave
once eleven
la oruga caterpillar
el oso marrón brown bear

la oveja sheep
el pájaro bird
el pan bread
el pantalón trousers
la papa potato
el papel paper
la pasta pasta
el pato duck
el pegamento glue
el perro dog
el pescado fish (to eat)
el pez fish (in the sea)
el pijama pajamas
la piña pineapple
el plátano banana
el plato dish
la playa beach
la pluma pen
el prado field
la profesora teacher
el puente bridge
el ratón mouse
la roca rock
rojo/roja red
la ropa clothes
seis six
septiembre September
la serpiente snake
siete seven
la silla chair
el sombrero hat
el supermercado supermarket
la televisión television
el tenedor fork
el tigre tiger
el tomate tomato
tres three
uno/una one
las uvas grapes
la vaca cow
el vaso glass
el velero sailboat
la ventana window
verde green
las verduras vegetables
el vestido dress
la zanahoria carrot
los zapatos shoes
el zorro fox